WILLY J. SMITH JR.

¿QUÉ PASÓ?

WHAT THE SPANISH BOOKS DON'T TEACH

Copyright © 2022 by Willie J. Smith, Jr.

All rights reserved. Printed in the United States of America. No part of this book may be used or reproduced in any manner whatsoever without written permission except in the case of brief quotations embodied in critical articles or reviews.

For information contact Authors Inside
P.O. Box 293, Oceano, CA 93475
Email: info@authorsinside.org
Website: www.authorsinside.com

ISBN: 978-1-954736-27-6
First Edition: November 2022

PRIMERA PARTE

¿Que Pasó?

What happened?

This is something I ask myself every day.

What happened?

I used to be so sure that I could speak Spanish so easily that I never doubted within a few months people would ask me whether I was Cuban or Puerto Rican.

¿Que Pasó?

It has been 11+ years and I still can't hold a decent conversation in Spanish. True, words came and come to me easily. True, I remember them much of the time. Yet, I have not done the one thing required of someone attempting to learn another language...speak.

How is that even possible?

Fear!

When I'd hear a Spanish-speaking person speak, I'd repeat a certain palabra (word) they'd use when talking to me, then I'd put it away. Sometimes a year would pass before I'd use that palabra again.

¿Que Pasó?

There were even *Palabras* (words) that I heard as a kid, not so nice words, that I could recall as an adult but felt these *Palabras* should be said with other Blacks or my Mexican friends who knew them. Prior to the year 2007, I'd never even thought about learning Spanish. A few incidents took place that made me consider and then finally decided to learn Spanish.

Uno: Training Day (the movie)

Dos: Cuba, a guy I liked as a person but who spoke no English and I almost hurt him over a misunderstanding.

Tres: History (Afro-Latinos)

Cuatro: Haters (enemigos), people who didn't want me to learn Spanish, even fear, which I alluded to earlier.

Fear of looking stupid in the eyes of Spanish speakers.

Fear of not measuring up to my family's standards.

That fear surfaced when I realized it wouldn't be as easy as I thought, and I feared some people would deceive/misguide me on purpose. With that, let's look at how this journey began.

Willy J. Smith, Jr.

I arrived at Calipatria State Prison in 1999. Having a love for music and not being able to watch any type of English videos, I watched Spanish ones. Learning all of the biggest names in Spanish music, and knowing about the songs they sang, people began to inquire and ask me, *¿Hablas español?*

It was understandable, but no, I did not speak Spanish. I was just enjoying the music videos. I didn't need to know Spanish for that. As I think back on it, even I'm surprised this wasn't enough to spur me into learning it.

No, the movie "Training Day" with Denzel Washington did that., I saw that movie 3 times in Spanish before I saw it in English and I desired, *muchísimo*, to know what they were talking about. It had more to do with the role that Denzel played in this movie. Nevertheless, I was bitten.

¿Que Pasó?

Cuba:

With that in mind, I had yet to go out in search of Spanish words or lessons. I would remember words that I'd heard around the yard, which were few, and said them to myself until I felt comfortable with a *Paisa* to use the *palabra* with him.

It was an incident with a guy called, "Cuba," while working in the kitchen, that finally forced me to look for help. Everyone called him Cuba because he was from Cuba. That's one of the tags you receive in prison. Even if people know your *Nombre* (name), we will still refer to you according to where you're from.

Now, normally, Cuba and I got along well. Even without knowing each other's language, other than his profuse use of English curse words (which everyone laughed at) we never had any problems.

Cuba was a little guy, maybe 120 lbs., and older than me. I was 33 years old at the time, busting down (working out), every day and moving like a 19-year-old.

I had gone to the serving line after asking one of the other Hispanic guys to use their cleaning supplies to clean my area. Cuba, not knowing this, immediately began to protest, saying, "Mine! Mine! Mine!"

No matter how much I tried to explain that one of his co-workers gave me permission, between his yells of "mine!" and my growing frustration, I kept coming up short. I noticed that a crowd was forming, so I asked one of the Hispanics to *explícale* (explain to him), what I was saying.

They refused, saying, "We don't understand him."

"You all speak Spanish!" I said, growing irate with the situation, "what are you talking about?"

While we were caught up in this crazy exchange, Cuba began tugging my arm, still yelling, "Mine!" I got angry and shoved him into the wall that we were standing beside.

I immediately became so full of shame that after the incident I began looking for a Spanish book to teach myself Spanish. Upon hearing me ask people for books, my co-workers, Fluto (out of Watts) and K.B. from the I.E., joined me in this endeavor.

K.B. knew someone who had some Spanish books they wanted to get rid of. The book we chose happened to use the "Berlitz Method." Since the chapters were so small, we decided on reading one chapter a week.

Being very undisciplined mentally, I found this very *difícil* (difficult), at first. It seemed

¿Que Pasó?

like one of us fell off every week and had to be encouraged to start again.

Willy J. Smith, Jr.

Of course, I had a few brothers from Mexico who tried to help me but, I didn't trust people like that, so, I always feared they were being dishonest, possibly. Then, there was my fear that if Hispanic gang members knew I spoke Spanish I would become a target in a prison riot, which I was assured was a reality on the Level IV yard.

So, keeping it to myself, I failed to verbalize those lessons which are paramount when it comes to learning a new language. K.B. was the only one amongst us who didn't have this problem. They couldn't shut him up. He spoke to everybody, even to people he knew who hated us speaking Spanish. He even got a Puerto Rican cellmate that would write him sentences.

I attribute this to his willingness to be open. Whereas I could read a little, I couldn't speak Spanish at all. It would be *muchos años* (many years) before I would be able to speak in Spanish. As for K.B., I have no doubt as to him being fluent in Spanish. I would be surprised if he were not.

¿Que Pasó?

Fortunately, a common and unfortunate event that takes place in prison – lockdown – allowed me to finish reading the book on my own. In the process, I learned some very profound lessons about myself.

1. I was a poor student
2. It feels good accomplishing something difficult *(difícil)*
3. I felt surprisingly peaceful and stable afterward, and
4. You must speak it

It was a struggle learning Spanish at the beginning. During the lockdown, I slept with that Spanish book. I read it upon awakening, I went to sleep reading it, and I repeated this process every day for the 8 or so months that we were on lockdown, and it paid off.

It wasn't until we returned to the regular program, and I was able to interact with my Mexican friends that I realized how much I still didn't know. Also, I realized that my fears would imprison me longer than I'd care to think about. So, I didn't. I continued to hide, study, and stagnate myself.

History:

The more I tended to my other studies of history and religion, I met Spanish speakers from other *países* (countries); Cuba, Puerto Rico, Panama, Belize, etc...., and began to learn that we came through the Islands before we came to America (slavery).

These guys would share with me their knowledge of our shared history. Surprisingly, they had so many roots (music, religion, food, language), that at times I'd feel embarrassed that this "foreigner" knew more about me than I did.

I would later come to accept them as my brothers, dads, and kinfolk from another master's plate. And being that women are such a big part of my life; I loved the idea of being able to love and learn through them what they see of the world.

I would walk the different prison yards learning from the different brothers what they had gone through in their own countries (*países*), what they believed they brought to this country and their experiences here.

¿Que Pasó?

I was no longer just learning Spanish. I was learning about people's lives. I was learning that many of their lives were/are connected to mine. That our hearts were linked together by an undeniable culture that seemed to be severed by languages and continents. Yet, there we were, being reconnected by my willingness to learn *otro lenguaje*.

How could I know that so many pieces of my future, my present, and my past were hidden from me by my ignorance? These people were closer to Africa than me. They had been reared with the knowledge of who they were, and for every 2 that aided me, I met another hater.

Haters (Enemigos)

These people were/are relentless. Cops, inmates, free staff, some of my own people, and more surprising than any, me. I allowed the way they felt about Blacks learning Spanish to stunt my development. My instinct was to fight back, so at times, I hated them for hating me.

Willy J. Smith, Jr.

It took me a long time to realize and eventually straighten out this defect. To not care what people thought and/or *dicho* (said), was more difficult than I thought it would be because this wasn't about Spanish...this was about self-development.

Dealing with haters taught me what Spanish speakers think about Blacks. Some things were good, some bad, and some things were stereotypical B.S. I was really challenged at times to hold my tongue.

Sometimes I got angry, spoke out against them, confided in others, laughed at their prejudice, and arrogantly flaunted my grasp of the *lenguaje,* which they considered their own and therefore, off limits. But mostly I was just humbled that so many were willing to share with me what they had.

I realized that it was mostly my own responses, and eventually, that retarded my growth in learning Spanish. When my Spanish-speaking friends would warn me that "staying in the books" instead of speaking interactively would slow my progress, I didn't trust them. So, for many years I continued to struggle.

¿Que Pasó?

Some were justified in their negative responses to my learning Spanish. I can admit that as a form of war, having your perceived enemy capable of decoding your language puts you at a disadvantage. For this reason, I sought to conceal that I was learning to speak Spanish from the start.

As for some of my people, especially in a prison setting, it could be seen as one not wanting to be Black, but something else. To be looked at as an enemy within could at times be fatal. Fortunately, I had the Creator and people who liked learning to validate my position. I was just a "brother" who liked learning, and due to this, people opened their arms to me.

The rest was all me. The shadows. The attitudes. My own mental laziness. The distrust of others. My drive for perfection and my fears that I might not measure up, all of these contributed to a laborious process.

SEGUNDA PARTE

¿Que Pasó?

Most times, I found it difficult to find good, basic Spanish books that teach you the fundamentals in a good way.

Also, as I learned, I attempted to show other guys (*otras personas*), who had wanted to learn Spanish. Part of my mistake was attempting to teach them (*enseñarlos*) from the books that I'd learned from, in the exact same manner I had learned.

We would both become frustrated after so many tries. Sooner or later, one of us would just give up. What I've learned in the process is that most of the guys that I was trying to teach were just like me, bad students.

Most of us never got out of high school. Not because we were dumb. We just lacked focus. The differences between us were, I had a passion for learning the subject I was afraid to quit, and I'd been in the water longer than the others.

By this I mean, I had already been chided by my friends for my lack of discipline and focus. I can truly admit now what I had failed to

¿Que Pasó?

admit then, due to my foolish pride, that they were right.

Prior to my attempts at learning Spanish, I had not followed any form of discipline on my own, nor had I been forced to, which I was becoming accustomed to in prison. Yet, I found myself frowning upon the lack of discipline all around me.

I looked at exercise, which is a given in prison, and our daily commitment to it, as a discipline. Especially when the circumstances aren't so favorable for optimal conditioning every day and you still must find ways to keep yourself motivated.

This is nothing compared to the ability to acquire the mental discipline necessary to accomplish something as tedious and arduous as learning *El language do otros personas* (other people's language) from other books.

I didn't quite understand the difficulties which lay ahead. I had always had a problem with being able to focus. This I knew (*lo sabía*). The problem began after being smacked across the forehead with a bat when I was a kid (*yo era joven*).

¿Que Pasó?

It was the summer before the start of the 4th grade and my uncle Patrick, who was a couple of years older than me, was trying to teach me to play baseball.

As I stood behind him, slightly to his left, trying to get a good view of his position and swinging technique, I was surprisingly overcome by the sudden impact of the bat to my forehead, and the pain that followed.

It took me *muchos años* (many years) and many problems, due to the intense look that I wore from trying to concentrate, which people often mistake for me having an attitude, for me to figure this out.

Up until that point, I thought I had a learning disability, and the face, which where I come from is called a "mad dog" can cause more problems than I care to annunciate.

At any rate, what I didn't understand at the time was, learning "Spanish" and learning "Spanish grammar" are two different things, and I was learning "Spanish grammar."

For those who don't know what grammar is and how painstakingly *dificil* (difficult) it is for a person like me (como yo), to learn. Imagine reading books about how to build houses and building a house while living in it. As opposed to just renting or buying a house – that's what I was attempting to do.

Because I had no reference to go on with grammar, I was ill-prepared to understand what I was about to go through. At first, it was cool, and I was very *emocionado* (excited) to be learning something new. The words and structure were pretty easy (*facil*) to understand. The masculine and feminine words for "the", particles they are called, "*el*" and "*la*," were easy to follow.

Words like *libro* (book), *gato* (cat), *caja* (box), pronounced CA-HA, and *pluma* (pen), was easy enough to understand and remember, as these were things I could see and say every day just as easily. But I wasn't saying the words. I was seeing them, and that was the problem.

Imagine my frustration at being able to pick these words out when I heard native Spanish speakers around me. Yet, not able to make sense of it. This is when the discipline began to kick in.

¿Que Pasó?

I had to really dig deep to find the focus that I would need to learn new Spanish words. I had to focus on sentence structure, recall, pay attention to people when they spoke, and respond accurately and in a timely manner. The last part, I'd failed to do for years.

In the process, I discovered another problem; one of the reasons I'd been having problems understanding the Spanish speakers around me is evidently I was learning proper Spanish and most of the people are me were not. By this I mean, most of the Hispanics born and raised in Southern California, and some *Paisas* (Mexicans).

I would've known this sooner had I trusted others enough to confide in someone. Even though, I think that had less to do with it than my own failure to apply what I'd learned. Had I engaged someone, anyone, I probably would've learned about this discrepancy *hace muchos años* (many years ago).

I had no problems reading Spanish, but every time I would speak it, I'd literally feel something inside of me refuse to move.

An emotion that until this day I can't figure out why it was there, where it came from, or why I allowed it to keep me from succeeding at speaking. There was such a level of irritation that accompanied it when doing so that I would stop trying to speak it for months at a time. Overcoming this became another challenge.

It's crazy how many things I was discovering about myself trying to learn Spanish. Also, I noticed some of those issues in the people around me.

I began to wonder if these things added to or were somehow responsible, in some ways, for our criminal leanings. Instead of voicing this to anybody, I began to apply this theory to the people I taught, without expressing *directamente* (directly), whether I believed it was good or bad, right or wrong, a part of our environment, or something innate.

I applied this theory to myself, also (*también*). What I have found out is that there was/is a profound connection, on so many levels, in my case.

- Being undisciplined
- Lack of focus
- Inconsistency, and
- Failure to make long-term commitments

¿Que Pasó?

Being undisciplined:

Maybe due to my inability to focus well, or due to the fact that I was spoiled growing up as a kid, I never had to be seriously responsible. Someone was always around to take up the slack. This allowed me to live freely, without any responsibilities at all.

I guess prison is the first serious thing to happen to me that I couldn't pawn off on someone else. Learning to deal with it has been a great challenge, but I believe, one that was necessary. Also, I believe that my irresponsibility has led to a default in other areas of my life.

Lack of focus:

A lack of focus ensures that I take on small projects. I had not yet learned to strengthen my focus enough to be able to work on what I had. Meaning, I had not learned (*no he aprendido*), how to maximize my potential with the focus that I had.

I hadn't had a serious understanding of myself in order to evaluate my strengths and weaknesses, at the time. Nor had anyone around me evaluated me, in a sense that would indicate that there was any real problem (*problema*).

Probably because we are all in the same boat.

¿Que Pasó?

I can say that learning Spanish in the way that I've been learning, has helped me greatly. It has taught me to be more systematic and disciplined in my approach to things. I was never this way prior to studying Spanish. It has truly been an invaluable experience.

Inconsistency:

Has taught me to be more consistent. One can't study grammar without being consistent. Grammar is not something one gets immediately (*inmediatamente*). It takes time. Depending on one's ability to focus and be disciplined enough to commit, it can sometimes take years.

Making long-term commitments:

Being consistent is something I have really had to work hard at. Because what's the reward for being consistent, over long periods of time, if it doesn't pay off?

I would rather spend my time enjoying things that I can see take shape immediately than spend a lot of useless time doing things I was not sure would come to fruition. This was my thinking back then (*hace mucho anos*).

I could not see the benefit of doing one thing for too long. I surely couldn't identify with anything enough to give it all of my time. This experience has taught me the value of being consistent in my commitments.

True, sometimes you can't ascertain what is around the corner until you turn it, and sometimes, it's not about what's around a corner so much as it is about the journey.

In my case, I've had many ups and downs on this road. Some things I feel like I could have done without, but then, the journey would not have been as interesting.

¿Que Pasó?

So, ¿Qué pasaba?

Well, I've learned to trust a little more. Since this had more to do with me than it had with others, the more I learned to trust myself, the less I had to worry about anyone else.

I learned that the prison you create for yourself could be worse than the prison that others put you in.

To receive the full benefit, I had to open myself up, wholly, to the process. Also, along the way, I learned to speak a little Spanish.

Other Books Published by Authors Inside

www.ingramcontent.com/pod-product-compliance
Lightning Source LLC
Chambersburg PA
CBHW071232160426
43196CB00012B/2489